Parentply

Rachel Murrill & Rachel Bright

Authentic

LONDON ● COLORADO SPRINGS ● HYDERABAD

First published 2007 by Authentic Media,
9 Holdom Avenue, Bletchley, Milton Keynes, Bucks, MK1 1QR, UK
1820 Jet Stream Drive, Colorado Springs, CO80921, USA
OM Authentic Media, Medchal Road, Jeedimetla Village, Secunderabad 500 055, A.P., India

Authentic Media is a division of IBS-STL UK, a company limited by guarantee (registered charity no. 270162)

For the purposes of this course, the word 'parent' refers to the primary care giver.

British Library Cataloguing in Publication Data
A catalogue record for this book is available from the British Library

ISBN 978-1-86024-592-3

Cover design by fourninezero design.
Print management by Adare.
Printed and bound by LPC Printing Ltd.

Contents

Parentplay

Acknowledgements

Thanks are due to Steve Murrill for his poem 'Shopping'; to New Life Church North, Milton Keynes, for their support and encouragement; to all the parents who have been willing to share their experiences; and to our faithful volunteers, who have given their time and energy to Parentplay.

A massive thank you also to our children, Ben, Alice and Ethan Murrill, and Elliana and Finn Bright, without whom none of this would have been possible (or necessary!).

Parentplay

About the Authors

 **Rachel Murrill** is a qualified Occupational Therapist, who has specialised in paediatrics, with over eleven years' experience. In the past six years she has been working in adult education, training professionals and volunteers in running groups and supporting parents. As a mother of three, she has always been passionate about parenting and parent support.

 **Rachel Bright** has been an enthusiastic advocate of parenting issues since she pioneered a support group and information service network for young parents after the birth of her first child in 1999. Following her move to Milton Keynes and birth of her second child she has been involved in many aspects of parent support, and is currently leading a large church youth work department.

As Christians looking to support other parents, they wanted to find a parenting course, aimed at the early-years age group, that would encourage and inspire parents. They were unable to find a course that had an emphasis on the practical aspects of play and that was accessible to the abilities and needs of the families in their local communities.

Therefore, Rachel and Rachel have co-written, run and trained others in using this unique, seven-week Parentplay course, which has seen great success over the past four years.

For further information on Parentplay visit our website www.parentplay.co.uk

Parentplay

Course Manual

Why Use Parentplay?

Parentplay is a fun, seven-week parenting course focusing on parents of children under 5. It depends to a large extent on informal, small group discussions followed by parents and children sharing an exciting messy-play time together.

Parentplay focuses on the needs of children and their parents. It is play-centred and is, therefore, lots of fun. The shared experience of the messy-play time, allows the opportunity for parents to put into practice some of the principles and new ideas they have learnt during the course.

'I feel reassured that I am doing a good job as a parent.'

Parentplay is committed to seeing family relationships develop. We believe that healthy relationships are crucial to children's healthy growth and development. Parentplay is specifically designed to be easily accessible to families with varying levels of ability and need. It is devised to be user-friendly for both facilitators and parents.

Parentplay Aims

Parentplay aims to strengthen family bonds and promote positive family relationships.

- Parentplay helps parents and children to feel valued and respected.

- Parentplay builds on parents' strengths as they learn new skills together by sharing ideas and experiences, enabling them to be positive role models for their children.

- Parentplay encourages parents and children to have fun together, developing a deeper bond, through a range of stimulating messy-play activities.

- Parentplay facilitates parents in building friendships and supporting one another, as a key to being actively involved in community life and all the benefits that this brings.

'Now I can step back and see what really matters.'

Parentplay

Session Topics

Session 1
RECHARGING YOUR BATTERIES
Helping parents to recognise the importance of taking care of their own needs, as well as those of their children.

Session 2
WHAT'S LOVE GOT TO DO WITH IT?
Exploring practical ways of showing and telling children that they are loved.

Session 3
I'M ALL EARS!
Developing effective listening skills.

Session 4
IT'S MORE THAN WORDS
Exploring the effects of labelling, shouting and saying sorry.

Session 5
WHY PLAY?
Inspiring parents to enjoy sharing play with their children and discover new ways of joining in.

Session 6
BALANCING WITH BOUNDARIES
Considering the reasons behind challenging behaviour, and strategies to set boundaries to deal with it appropriately.

Session 7
REMEMBER, REMEMBER!
Discussing the importance of building positive memories and valuing times together.

How to Use the Parentplay Material

Introduction

The Parentplay manual, with CD-ROM, contains all the materials and facilitators' notes necessary to run a parenting course for parents of children under 5. Each of the seven sessions should last approximately 2 hours.

The format for each session is as follows:
- Parents arrive and settle their children into the crèche
- Refreshments for parents
- Informal small group discussions (1$\frac{1}{2}$ hrs)
- Collect children from crèche
- Messy-play time for all to enjoy together
- Goodbye song

Session Plans

The course session plans are at the back of this manual.

A list of resources needed for each week can be found at the beginning of each session plan.

The facilitators' session plans give step-by-step guidance on how to run each session. The explanations given to outline each activity are suggestions only and are not intended to be read word-for-word. This then gives you the freedom to explain the activities in a way that you feel is most appropriate to your group.

Weekly Handouts

These are a really useful tool to hand out to the parents towards the end of each session, to assist in transferring learning to their home. The handouts act as a helpful reminder to parents and, as a brief summary of the session, they can also be used to share the topics with partners/family who may not be able to attend. The weekly handouts also provide an opportunity to finish your session on an encouraging note.

It is crucial to leave sufficient time at the end of each session for parents to complete their action plan for the week and to share these with the group. Encourage parents to be specific in choosing realistic and achievable goals each week.

Each subsequent session begins with feedback on how each of their action plans have gone, which encourages accountability and mutual support.

These double sided A5 weekly handouts can be found on the Parentplay CD-ROM. We recommend printing these onto coloured card or paper, using a different colour for each week, and providing parents with an A5-sized plastic zip-wallet to keep their weekly handouts in.

Parentplay

The Parentplay CD-ROM

The CD-ROM contains copies of all the printed material that you will need when running your Parentplay course. The forms, letters and posters can all be customised to include your own course information. The CD-ROM includes:

Checklists
- Checklist for setting up a Parentplay course
- Checklist for Parentplay open morning

Publicity
- Open morning flyers and poster
- Course flyers and poster

Administration
- Welcome letter with session overview
- Course registration form
- Door signs
- Name badges
- Weekly attendance register
- Facilitators' weekly evaluation form
- Parents' end of course evaluation questionnaire
- Certificate of attendance

Course Materials
- Sun and cloud illustrations (for week 1)
- Agony Aunt Ethel letters (for week 3)
- Goldfish illustrations (for week 6)
- Handprints poem (for week 7)

Weekly Handouts 1–7

Can I Really Run a Parentplay Course?

Parentplay is designed to be run by parents, volunteers and professionals working with families. No particular qualifications are necessary.

The basic requirement is that you have an ability to empathise and get on well with parents. If you can be a 'cheerleader' to other parents, encouraging them on their journey as parents, then you qualify. The key is to be a 'facilitator' of the parents sharing in the discussion time, rather than a 'teacher' with all the answers.

'I've learnt so much.'

Please be aware that this course is not designed as an in-depth counselling course. You therefore need to be aware of other services you can refer parents on to, should the need arise.

How Does Parentplay Fit into Your Community?

Whether you are looking to run a Parentplay course as a professional in your place of work (e.g. family/health centre), within the voluntary sector (church, other faith groups, community centre, toddler group, or in your own home) or any other family support groups. Parentplay can be used to build and further develop contact with parents within your community, wherever that may be.

If your group is actively seeking to serve the local community, then running Parentplay courses is a great way of doing this.

'I don't feel so lonely now.'

Parentplay

Who to Invite?

The Parentplay course is best used with families who have children under the age of 5. However, whilst the principles of each session remain relevant to most age groups, the case studies and activities can be tailored to fit the ages of the children represented in your group. For example, if you have predominantly babies in your group, then activities and discussions can be tailored to enable these parents to get the most out of them.

'I felt so welcomed.'

Parentplay is designed to be used in a wide variety of groups with varying levels of ability and need. Your target group is likely to include your friends, family, neighbours, clients, local parent and toddler groups, local pre-schools, school nurseries, ante- and post-natal groups, to mention a few. It is helpful to think about who you would like to invite before you advertise, and then think about where those people are most likely to see or hear about your group.

It is important to consider how you will include different groups of people in your Parentplay course. For example, mothers, fathers, single parents, young parents and those from a variety of cultural backgrounds. These will need to be considered when planning your publicity, course material and activities, to ensure that people are included in the best way for them to get the most out of the course. You can find all the necessary publicity, flyers and posters for you to add your own details to, on the Parentplay CD-ROM included with this book.

It is worth remembering that although you are focusing on the 0–5 age group, some parents will also have older children, which they may want to discuss. At Parentplay we try our best to serve whole families, and obviously the needs of different family members affect each other. Therefore, we try to allow time for extended discussions, but also ensure that these do not dominate the whole group discussions. Individual families may need a separate time to gain help outside of the course sessions.

Open Morning

You may like to put on an open morning to invite prospective group participants to. This is a chance for them to see the kind of activities you do before they decide to enrol for the course. If you give people the chance to sign up at the open morning, it will also give you the opportunity to gauge how many people are likely to attend the course.

There is a checklist and flyers/posters (on the CD-ROM) to help you plan for an open morning as a taster session, should you wish to use these to advertise your course.

Group Size

We recommend that the best size for your group discussions is 8–12 people. This provides enough space for everyone to have a chance to contribute and feel heard. However, you may need to take account of some people missing sessions occasionally or dropping out altogether.

In order for the group to get the most out of the course we suggest not adding any new members to the group after the second session.

Obviously you will need to discuss with your crèche provider how many children, and what ages they can safely provide for. This will also affect how many parents can attend the course.

Parentplay

Practicalities

Health and Safety

We recommend that you aim for the highest possible standard of health and safety and take all necessary precautions at all times. Aspects to consider when thinking about your setting include:

- Safe and adequate heating
- Safe and appropriate height furniture
- Cleanable floor surfaces
- Plug socket covers
- Clear fire exits, fire procedures and extinguishers
- Adequate toilet and baby changing facilities
- Kitchen hygiene for serving of refreshments and messy-play food preparation
- Secure doors
- Lighting

It is important that children are given adequate supervision at all times. Ensure that parents are made aware that they are responsible for supervising their own children during the messy-play time.

It is good practice to have at least one first-aid-trained team member.

Insurance Cover

Check existing building insurance policies to ensure adequate cover.

Crèche

The Parentplay course is run during the daytime, so it will be neccesary to run a crèche to look after the children whilst the parents are in the discussion group.

You may have the resources to provide your own crèche. However this is not always possible, so you may have to hire a mobile crèche. Mobile crèches are easy to find – your local council will be able to give you details of crèches in your area.

Some of the children coming on your course may not have been separated from their parents before, so you may find some children and parents become anxious when they come to do this. It is worth having someone from your team on hand to offer reassurance and support to parents as they leave their children.

Child Protection

You may wish to notify your local authority of the group you are running but you are not required, at present, to officially register, as the crèche facility will run for less than 2 hours. However, it is good practice to ensure that all crèche helpers are checked by the Criminal Records Bureau (information line: 0870 90 90 811). Good practice (at time of publication) suggests crèche staffing ratios of :

1 staff : 3 children aged 0–2 years
1 staff : 4 children aged 2–3 years
1 staff : 8 children aged 3–6 years

Your organisation/community group should have its own guidelines for good practice and child protection policy when working with children and their recommendations should be followed.

Confidentiality

Your group agreement (which can be found on the weekly handout for Session 1) will generate discussion at your first session on the issues surrounding confidentiality and trust. Obviously these are essential to enable members of your group to feel relaxed and to share in a secure environment.

However, the nature of any parenting course is such that there may be disclosures of sensitive and personal information. You will need to have thought in advance about how you will handle these disclosures and be aware of other support services that may be available to parents, should the need arise.

It is essential for facilitators to include the issue of child protection, for example, using the wording provided in your plan for Session 1. If you are concerned about the well-being of any child or young person, you will need to discuss this with the parent/s and you may need to contact your local Social Services department.

Photography

Whilst most people who come in and out of your building will have children's best interests at heart, unfortunately, we need to be especially aware of the possibility that some visitors' intentions may be more sinister. For this reason, it is essential that photographs of any children are only taken after written consent from the parent, and are never displayed with their names attached in places where the general public have access.

We recommend using the Parentplay registration form (on the CD-ROM) to request a parent's signature to give permission to take photos of their children during the session, indicating that these may be used for publicity.

At Parentplay we do our best to take lots of photographs, from which we select one of each child to put in a simple frame to be presented to the parent, by their child, at the end of the course. This surprise gift has been very successful in giving the family a memento of their time at Parentplay.

Getting Ready

Preparation is essential to the smooth running of your Parentplay course. We recommend that you are thoroughly familiar with the course contents and resources before beginning your course.

Checklists

We have included sample checklists (on the CD-ROM) that you may find helpful in thinking about what you need to consider when setting up and running your Parentplay course.

Timings

We recommend doing some research to find out what time of day would be most appropriate to your target group, as this will influence who will be able to attend. You may particularly want to avoid times when other local groups are running, and school and pre-school pick-up times.

Always start your sessions at your advertised time. Sticking as closely as possible to the suggested timings will enable you to finish promptly, allowing plenty of time for the messy-play activities. We recommend that you have a visible clock in each room to help with this, and add your own timings (in pencil) to your session plans.

Venue

You will need a minimum of two rooms, and ideally three rooms, in order to run your Parentplay course. One will be needed for the crèche and one for the group discussions. Try to make the parents' room as comfortable and informal as possible. It is also better if this room is not directly next to the crèche room.

You will also need a room for the messy-play time at the end. Obviously this room will need to be easily cleanable. If you do not have a third room for the messy-play time, you can double up its function with one of your other rooms but may need to allow some time after the discussions to set this up.

You will need to ensure that your venue is accessible for pushchairs and for those with disabilities. You may also need space to store pushchairs during the running of the course. Please ensure you familiarise yourself with fire and emergency procedures for the venue.

Your Team

We recommend running Parentplay with two people as co-facilitators of the group, although the discussion groups can be led by one person if necessary. You will need to assign roles between you as to who will:

- Publicise the course
- Book the venue and crèche
- Photocopy or print necessary course resources
- Organise the refreshments
- Prepare the messy-play activities
- Set up and clear away

Wherever possible, we suggest adding to your team and bringing in volunteers who can help with, for example, the refreshments and messy-play time. This will free you up to have more time to speak with the parents one-to-one.

We have found that some helpers who start off making coffee are now Parentplay co-facilitators, as we have given them more opportunities to learn and develop their own skills too.

As team leader it will make your job easier if you have made time to do the following:

- Ensure your team members have read this manual.
- Plan together, in advance, who is going to do what.
- Add timings to your session plans.

Budgeting

Be sure to budget adequately for running the course. Funding will be needed for:

- Rent of rooms
- Photocopying and printing of resources
- Publicity
- Postage
- Refreshments – sharing food together is a great ice-breaker so be creative (e.g., home-made cakes, pastries, bacon butties)
- Messy-play equipment
- Memory boxes (one for each child)
- Crèche

Keep records of income and expenditure with proof of purchases.

We recommend charging a minimal amount to cover costs, for example £1 per child, per week. Most parents are more than willing to contribute towards something that they and their children can enjoy and learn from together. However, we do ask you to be sensitive to those for whom even a nominal charge is too much, as we would not want anyone to miss out because of the cost.

Parentplay

Funding

Parentplay has been designed to be run on a minimal budget. However, if you do require funding, here are some things to consider:

- Research what kinds of funding/charitable grants are available in your local area that you may be able to benefit from.
- Attend local funding fairs, contact agencies that support voluntary groups and local council parenting providers groups, your local CVO (council for voluntary organisations) and Adult Continuing Education centre, to find out how they can support and advise you with funding issues.
- Visit local libraries, which may have details of local and national charities that may be able to offer funding.
- Make sure you establish whether or not you fit the criteria before you make an application and always read the small print. Always check with your leadership/management committee that they are happy for you to pursue outside funding. Be equipped with a clear plan of action.
- Remember to consider the conditions placed on any funding, so as not to compromise your core values and beliefs.

Evaluation

Evaluating each session is important in order to review what has gone well and help you plan any changes you may want to make. Weekly evaluation sheets for you to record both your and parents' comments can be found on the Parentplay CD-ROM.

An overall course evaluation completed by the parents will give you valuable information about what they have gained from and enjoyed on the course. This will also give you suggestions of ways to improve your future Parentplay courses.

A Parentplay end-of-course evaluation form to give to your parents, can be found on the CD-ROM. We recommend that you print these in colour, and make them double-sided so they appear less daunting for parents to complete. The blank boxes on page two allow space for you to type or write your own suggestions as to what your parents may want to express an interest in (for example, a reunion, support group, other courses, etc.).

Record Keeping

A record of who is in the building is needed for fire and emergency procedures. This also serves as an attendance record. (This can be printed from the CD-Rom.)

It is helpful to keep records of addresses, telephone numbers and emergency contacts. However, in keeping within the bounds of the data protection act, information should remain confidential and should not be divulged to any third parties.

Storage

A lot of the messy-play resources can most usefully be shared with other groups who may already be using the building, e.g. toddler or pre-school groups. However, you will need storage for things like:

- Flipchart
- Extra messy-play resources
- Stationery/administration resources
- Small tables and chairs

We therefore recommend that you try to negotiate some storage space!

Parenting Library

If you have time and resources it is helpful to have a selection of books on various parenting topics for parents to borrow during the course. Remember to include some CDs and DVDs, too, if you can.

Resource Guide

Often parents ask where they can find out about parent/family related information, for example, 'Where is my local playgroup?' 'What can I do about my child's ezcema?' 'Are there any cheap places to go and play?'

If you have time to collect any leaflets on these kinds of resources in your locality, it will make your job easier, in the long term, to be able to offer informed suggestions and advice.

Handling Tricky Situations

It would be impossible to prepare you for every eventuality of what might happen in your groups. However well you prepare for your sessions, there may be times when you face challenges, when difficult situations arise. You do need to be aware that individuals will come to your Parentplay courses with their own personalities, agendas, issues and perspectives. Examples of this might be a parent who is over-contributive or domineering, an emotional outburst, a parent who is consistently late … to mention but a few. This may sometimes cause difficulty in your group dynamics or may hamper some individuals from progressing as much as you would like within your group.

Here are a few guidelines for dealing with some of these difficult situations:

- It is important to create a secure and trusting environment where parents feel confident to share. Enforcing and referring to the group agreement can help in developing this.
- Do your best to discover the underlying reason for the behaviour. This will help you to identify possible ways of dealing with it.
- Try not to take it personally. Be willing to listen to constructive criticism but be sure to listen to the positives too.
- Be sure to actively listen to all contributions, giving your full attention.
- Do not allow parents to openly criticise or undermine one another's parenting.
- Always show respect for the individual even though you may not agree with their opinions or behaviour.

Children's Behaviour

Do

- Make sure parents are aware that they are responsible for their children during the session.
- Help the parents and your team to develop positive ways of dealing with common problems such as biting, not sharing, tantrums, etc.
- Encourage parents to deal with difficult behaviour positively.
- Have clear guidelines on how you will deal with difficult behaviour during the crèche times.

Don't

- Discuss a child's behaviour in front of the child or other children.
- Intervene in how a parent is parenting their child, unless asked to do so or if a child is at risk of harm.

Messy-Play Activities

The following provides you with seven messy-play activity ideas to accompany the seven-week Parentplay course. There are also three extra suggestions for alternatives which you may like to substitute.

We have found that it is best to set up the activity prior to everyone arriving, to save time in-between the discussion and messy-play times. It is best to select activities so that there isn't something to take home every week, and vary the activities that require the most clearing up, so that you're not worn out every week!

We have tried to include as many activities as possible that can be done with babies. Messy-play sessions should be focused on the children taking part. The parents should be encouraged to focus on their own children rather than what others are doing. Messy-play is not a competition – the aim is not to decorate the perfect cake or make the best picture but to have fun!

We suggest you choose the seven activities that best suit your setting and resources, and the ones you think will be most fun for you and the children. After all, that's what it's all about! We are sure that you will have lots of ideas of your own, too. Please feel free to use them and let us know how they work. We are always looking for new ideas!

The Purpose of Messy-Play Time

- The messy-play time provides the opportunity for parents and children to have quality time together, especially doing activities that they wouldn't always get the chance to try at home. Do encourage parents to join in with their children doing the activity, without taking over. Suggest that the end result is less important than the time taken to do the activity together.
- It gives parents a chance to immediately put into practice what they may have learnt during the discussion time, e.g. listening to their child, or sharing their child's playtime without taking over.
- It is a great reward for the children after being separated from their parents during crèche.
- The messy-play time also gives you, as the facilitator, the opportunity to support parents in learning how to enjoy sharing play with their children. Modelling good parenting is a very valuable tool. Get stuck in! If you're having fun, it will be infectious. Have a laugh together, it's good for you all!

'I've learnt to spend more quality time with my children.'

Parentplay

Messy-Play Practicalities

- Allow a minimum of 30 minutes for messy-play each week. You may need to allow a little more time on the last celebration week.
- You will need sufficient floor covering and an apron for each child. We suggest that you recommend to parents that they bring their children dressed in old clothes or bring a change of clothes for them if they prefer. For this reason it is best not to choose too messy an activity for Session 1.
- You may have a scrap store in your area run by the Play Association. These are great for getting cheap messy-play resources.
- No child should be forced by their parents to join in, as some children dislike getting messy. It is better for them to join in on whatever level they are comfortable, in order for them to enjoy the session.
- Think about how to set out the room, to encourage adults to join in with their children, e.g. no adult chairs.
- We have found it helpful to explain the purpose of the messy-play time to the parents in order to encourage them to participate fully, understanding why they are given opportunity for quality time with their children.
- If at all possible it is a good idea to make space for drying work and to offer to dry any paintings, which can then be taken home after the next week's session – they never look the same by the time they get home otherwise!
- It is a good idea to write children's names on their work. This saves considerable time trying to work out whose is whose at the end of the session!

Messy-Play for Young Babies

It is not easy to include young babies in all activities. However, it is vital that you encourage parents to be confident enough to allow their babies to explore and get messy.

Some ideas may include:

- Cooking – let them explore textures when cooking, mixing with hands, tasting.
- Painting – let them explore the texture of brushes, sponges, rollers, vegetables, etc. and also let them use suitable finger paints.
- Water-play – shallow trays with a little water for dropping objects in or patting with hands; blowing bubbles or using a bubble machine.
- You may like to organise a separate multi-sensory baby section, where babies get the opportunity to explore different textures (e.g. silk scarves, sponges), sights and sounds.

Session 1: Water-Play

It is best to provide a variety of water-play activities for the children to move around and do with their parents. This helps maintain their interest.

Resources needed:
- Plastic items to wash up in bowls on a table. Put bubble bath in the water.
- Large water trays with bottles, buckets, water wheels, etc. for pouring.
- Paddling pool for getting feet wet using watering cans and general bath toys.
- Dollies to bath in bowls of water.
- Sea creatures in a bowl of dark green water (use food colouring).
- Baking trays with a tiny amount of water for splashing ducks into, or for driving plastic cars around in. Babies love just patting their hands in water to make splashes.
- Small tables and coverings
- Small chairs
- Aprons
- Bubble machine

Suggestions:
- Vary the height of different activities to add appeal
- Have lots of towels on hand
- Mop up regularly to help prevent accidents
- Get in the paddling pool yourself
- Adding nice-smelling bubbles adds to the sensory experience
- We recommend that you beg and borrow a lot for this week. It's amazing how many water trays and toys you can round up from family and friends, saving the need to buy lots of toys for this session.

Points to watch out for:
- Wet floors can be very dangerous, ensure you have adequate plastic floor coverings or newspapers.
- Obviously no child should be left unsupervised – a child can drown in a very small amount of water.
- Children with sensitive skin will probably need water without bubbles or colouring.
- Make sure you keep the room warm enough for the children to get wet and still feel comfortable.

Parentplay

Session 2: Cooking

Children love eating what they have made. There are lots of different options for a cooking week, and many of these will depend on whether you have the facilities to cook/heat food or not. We have included a few of our suggestions, however the options are endless, so use your imagination.

- **Chapattis** – Indian bread that can be prepared by the parents and children together, and then be quickly cooked by adults in a frying pan in a couple of minutes.
- **Mini Pizzas** – small ready-made pizza bases can be bought from supermarkets, so you can just prepare a selection of toppings for children to decorate their pizza. These can then be cooked at the time (in 10 minutes) or at home.
- **Crispy Cakes** – these are very quick and easy to prepare and can be made seasonal by adding toppings, e.g. mini eggs on top to make Easter nests.
- **Fridge Cake** – again these are quick but fun to make with no oven needed; they just need to be refrigerated once the children are back at home.

Resources needed:
- Small tables and coverings
- Aprons
- Small chairs
- Hand-washing bowl and paper towels
- Ingredients and recipes
- Wooden spoons and other equipment for mixing
- Containers/plates to take food home
- Pen to write names
- Anti-bacterial spray to clean tables beforehand.

Suggestions:
- You may want to give parents a recipe sheet with the recipes you have used in the sessions (or other simple, inexpensive recipes) to do with their children at home.
- Encourage parents to bring in the recipes they use at home to share with other parents.
- Encourage the children to do as much of the activity for themselves as they can, e.g. adding ingredients, stirring, spooning out and so on.
- You may like to take time to let the children decorate or make their own baskets, containers or plates, too.

Points to watch out for:
- If you have young babies in the group, you might like to include some foods that they can just enjoy exploring, even though there will be no end result to take home, e.g. baked beans in a tray, cooked spaghetti, jelly, etc. This is a great way for babies to enjoy messy-play with their parents, without worrying about them putting things in their mouths.
- Please make sure that you are aware of any relevant allergies and do not include products that may contain nuts.

Session 3: Hand and Foot Painting

We recommend providing a variety of painting activities to cover a range of ages and maintain interest. Children and parents can move around the different activities and children should be encouraged to join in all of them. However, no child should be forced to join in. Some children find hand and foot painting too messy to tolerate, so you might like to provide brushes and other implements for them to use instead.

We suggest that you do your best to find somewhere to store drying paintings so they can be taken home on the following week.

General resources needed:
- Floor mats
- Small tables covered with mats or newspaper
- Small chairs
- Hand-washing table and paper towels
- Foot-washing bowl on floor next to foot painting activities
- Drying rack or airer
- Pencil to write names
- Aprons

A variety of the following can be used:

1. HAND AND FOOT PRINTS (to laminate and give to parents at the end of the course)

Resources needed:
- White paper
- Paint in trays (big enough to fit hands and feet into)

At a later date you will need:
- Poem printed from CD-ROM (onto coloured A4 paper)
- Glue to stick hand and foot prints onto the poem
- Laminator and pouches

Parentplay

Poem and layout suggestion:

> Sometimes you get discouraged
> Because I am so small
> And always leave my fingerprints
> On furniture and walls
>
> But every day I'm growing –
> I'll be grown some day
> And all those tiny hand prints
> Will surely fade away
>
> So here's a little hand print
> Just so you can recall
> Exactly how my fingers looked
> When I was very small
> (Author unknown)

2. PAINTING TWO HAND PRINTS TOGETHER TO MAKE A BUTTERFLY
Resources needed:
- Coloured A5 paper
- Paint in trays large enough to fit hand in

3. FINGER PAINTING (e.g. painting dots onto a picture with finger tips)
Resources needed:
- Pre-drawn and photocopied pictures on coloured paper
- Pots of paint to dip fingers in

4. FOOT PAINTING (walking across large sheets of wallpaper)
Resources needed:
- Wallpaper
- Paint in trays large enough to stand in

5. PAINTING WITH LARGE BRUSHES
Resources needed:
- Paper
- Brushes
- Paint in pots

Points to watch out for:
- Be sure to use non-toxic and washable paints that are specifically designed for children.
- Trays of paint can be very slippery to stand on so please warn parents. Putting a spongy cloth on the tray before adding the paint can help make the paint less slippery.

Session 4: Music and Movement

This is a great fun session for parents and children to enjoy together. It's not strictly 'messy' but, halfway through the course you might appreciate one less messy session to clear up.

We suggest spending 5–10 minutes making some shakers and razzle-dazzle sticks (see below) with the older children, while the babies are helped to tie some colourful ribbons to plastic bracelets. These can then be used during the music time.

We recommend making a variety of musical 'instruments' together, for example:

SHAKERS
Resources needed:
- Plastic cups or bottles, brightly decorated
- Dry pasta to put into cups or bottles
- Paper circle to put over the top or bottle lids
- Sticky-tape to attach the paper circle to the cup
- Pens to write names
- Short lengths of ribbons to sticky-tape onto the bottom of the cup or bottle
- Stickers to decorate

RAZZLE-DAZZLE STICKS
Resources needed:
- Kitchen roll tube covered in brightly coloured paper
- Lengths of ribbon, crêpe paper, sparkly paper, etc. to stick into the top of the tube

RIBBON BRACELETS
Resources needed:
- Plastic bracelets
- Lengths of colourful ribbon to tie on

MUSIC TIME

1. Sit in a circle to sing a few action songs. Feel free to use pre-recorded tapes to sing along to if you prefer.

2. Dance around the room with shakers, razzle-dazzle sticks and ribbon bracelets to a piece of flouncy classical music. You could blow bubbles or use a bubble machine here, too.

3. Sing and play the musical instruments you have made to popular children's theme tunes, or try using everyday objects as instruments. This is a great one for showing parents that baking trays, saucepans, plastic bowls, wooden spoons and colanders can all be used to have fun at home . . . for free!

Parentpl♥y

Suggestions:

- Get stuck in and act daft yourself. It allows others to feel free to enjoy themselves and be a bit silly too!
- Another idea is to ask someone to come in to show, play and tell the children about some real instruments.
- Be creative and add puppets, multicultural instruments and so on.

Session 5: Painting

There are many things you can use to paint with, but here are some that we have found particularly successful. Again, as with the other weeks, we suggest that you provide a variety of activities so people can move around.

Resources needed:
- Vegetables (ready cut) – e.g. peppers, carrots, celery, sweet potatoes, yams – to make an interesting variety of shapes
- Shaped sponges
- Stencils
- Paint stamps
- Rollers
- Leaves, twigs or other things from nature
- Toy cars or tractors to make tyre-track patterns
- A5 paper in a variety of colours
- Luminous and/or white paint colours in small trays
- Small tables covered with mats or newspaper
- Small chairs
- Hand-washing table and paper towels
- Pencil to write names
- Aprons

Suggestions:
- The above painting methods can be used to make seasonal gift cards.
- If possible offer to dry paintings to be collected next week.
- This is a good week to do hand prints again, if anyone missed Session 3, to ensure that you have prints of every child to laminate with the poem to give as a surprise to the parents at the end of the course.

Parentplay

Session 6: Play Dough

Not only does making their own play dough add to the enjoyment for the children, it also demonstrates to the parents how to make dough at home. We suggest that you allow them to take home what they have made. You can either make uncooked dough (which does not keep) or cooked, depending on your resources. Here's a good recipe for cooked dough:

Resources needed:
- Saucepan
- 1 cup of salt
- 2 tablespoons of cooking oil
- 2 cups of plain flour
- Few drops of food colouring and/or flavourings

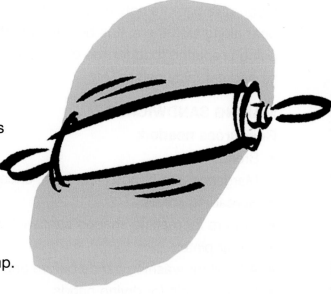

Method:
- Mix all the ingredients together in a saucepan.
- Cook over a medium heat, stirring all the time. The mixture will go like scrambled eggs and start to come away from the pan to form a lump.
- Remove from the heat, cool and knead.

This dough stores well in an airtight box.

Additional resources:
- Sequins or glitter to add to the dough
- Fragrance drops
- Small tables and chairs
- Cutters and rolling pins
- Food bags to take play dough home in
- Recipe sheets for parents to take home to be able to make more
- Plastic gloves for those with sensitive skin to wear

Suggestions:
- Allow time to make the play dough, and then time to play with it.
- Adding colour, texture (e.g. sequins) and smell to the play dough adds to the sensory experience.
- Be aware that some parents may need reassuring with some ideas of what to make and how to share the activity with their children.

Session 7: Celebration

We suggest that on the last week you give the messy-play time a party feel, to celebrate the end of the course. The session works particularly well as a teddy bears' picnic.

As this is a less messy week, you should get more opportunity to chat with the parents and enjoy the celebration as a group.

Teddy Bears' Picnic

If you give parents notice the week before, they can bring their child's favourite teddy bear along with them. It is best to split the session into two halves, with the first part being preparing food for the children to eat together, and the second part being a time to sit and eat, play games, etc.

MAKING SANDWICHES
Resources needed:
- Bread
- Margarine and fillings (jam, ham, cheese, etc.)
- Spreading knives
- Cutters for making shaped sandwiches
- Paper plates
- A bowl for washing hands before and afterwards
- Paper towels for drying hands
- Anti-bacterial spray to clean tables with beforehand

DECORATING CAKES AND/OR BISCUITS
Resources needed:
- Digestive biscuits
- Small fairy cakes
- Icing sugar, water, food colouring to mix
- Sweets, raisins and fruit for decoration
- Sieve
- Bowls and spoons for mixing
- Paper baskets/plates to put cakes or bisuits in to take home
- Pen to write names on baskets/plates
- A bowl for washing hands before and afterwards
- Paper towels for drying hands
- Anti-bacterial spray to clean tables with beforehand

Points to watch out for:
- Please make sure that you are aware of any relevant allergies and do not include products that may contain nuts.
- Provide options of more healthy decorations.
- Ensure any sharp knives are kept out of the reach of children.

Music

You could do some singing together, using the theme of teddy bears, or just ask the children for their favourite songs. Having background music on the rest of the time is a good idea, and makes for a fun atmosphere.

Face Painting

You can buy face paints in most children's toyshops. You only need a few colours, which you can then mix with small brushes. It is a good idea to have some pictures that you think you can paint, for the children to choose from.

Make sure you check for any skin allergies before applying face paints.

Parachute or Balloon Games

Children love parachute and balloon games and they add a real party feel as they are so big, bright and colourful. Many toddler groups/pre-schools will have a parachute you may be able to borrow, but they can be hired through such places as toy libraries.

Additional Messy-Play Ideas

1. STICKING ACTIVITIES

You could choose any kind of sticking activity. Children particularly like sticking different textures, e.g. pieces of paper and fabric, to make a collage. These could be made individually or the whole group could make one large collage to display somewhere.

You could also draw and photocopy a picture of a popular children's character for them to stick crêpe paper onto. A particularly good one to try is sticking squares of coloured crêpe paper onto a picture of Elmer the elephant from David McGee's stories.

Resources needed:

- Outline of Elmer the elephant already drawn on A3 sheets of white paper
- Squares of different coloured crêpe paper
- Pots of PVA glue or glue sticks (if you prefer to be less messy)
- Small tables and coverings
- Small chairs
- Aprons
- Bowl of water for hand washing

Suggestions:

- Children love the story of Elmer, so why not read it to them at the end? This will also provide you with the opportunity of showing parents how to share books with their children in a fun and exciting way.

2. CLAY HAND MODELLING

Parents love having keepsakes of their children. Using air-drying modelling clay, you can cut a large lump for each child to roll out, cut around a circular plate and make an imprint of their hand or foot. Pencils can be used to imprint their names or make a patterned edge.

Parentplay

Once these have dried they can be painted and varnished to keep as a memento of their childhood.

Resources needed:

- Clay cut into lumps
- Rolling pins
- Plates to cut around
- Cardboard to dry hand/foot prints on
- Tools for patterning and writing names and dates
- Hand-washing bowls and paper towels
- Paints a couple of weeks later

Suggestions:

Clay could also be used for making other models too.

3. SEASONAL ACTIVITIES

You may want to tailor some of your activities to the time of year. Christmas, Easter, Mother's Day, Father's Day and/or multicultural festivals may all be a source of inspiration as you plan your activities.

Be sure to let us know if you think of something new to add so we can share it with other people on the Parentplay website (www.parentplay.co.uk).

Home Time

A positive ending to every session brings about a sense of completion and anticipation of next week. It is an important signal to remind children that the session is coming to an end, and to prepare them for going home.

We recommend all sitting together to sing a 'goodbye song'. You could get a selection of carpet tiles or cushions so each child could sit on one. This is particularly good if the children find it difficult to stay sitting down.

We have found that children respond particularly well to having a puppet, for example Winnie-the-Pooh, who wakes up and comes out of his box when they call him to join in the song with them. Use the puppet and sing:

If you're happy and you know it clap with Pooh
If you're happy and you know it clap with Pooh
If you're happy and you know it and you really want to show it
If you're happy and you know it clap with Pooh

If you're happy and you know it jump with Pooh
If you're happy and you know it jump with Pooh
If you're happy and you know it and you really want to show it
If you're happy and you know it jump with Pooh

If you're happy and you know it wave goodbye
If you're happy and you know it wave goodbye
If you're happy and you know it and you really want to show it
If you're happy and you know it wave goodbye

'I can now look forward to the future.'

Parentplay

Parentpl⬤y
Session Plans

Key

 Where this appears, please put the information into your own words.

 Where this appears, there will be a practical illustration or activity for you to carry out with the group.

 Where this appears, briefly recap the previous week's session and ask parents to feed back what they have tried.

 Where this appears, there will be notes for you to bear in mind but not neccesarily share with the group.

 Where this appears, the whole group will share the discussion of a topic.

 Where this appears, the group will need to split into two or three smaller groups.

 Where this appears, the small group will feed back their ideas to the whole group.

 Where this appears, give out and refer to, the weekly handout for the relevant session.

Session 1
Recharging Your Batteries

Time: 2 hours

Aim:

To encourage parents to be the best they can be, by being themselves and taking care of their own needs as well as those of their children.

Learning Outcomes:

By the end of the session participants will be able to:

1. Understand the value of being a parent.

2. Appreciate themselves more as parents.

3. Demonstrate a greater awareness of their feelings as parents.

4. Practically plan how to meet their own needs.

You will need (in order of activity):

- [ ] Refreshments
- [ ] Name stickers and pens
- [ ] Calculator
- [ ] Ground rules

    (weekly handout 1 on CD-Rom)

- [ ] Sun and cloud cut-outs

    one of each for each person (on CD Rom)

- [ ] Large sun and cloud stuck

    onto flipchart paper (on CD Rom)

- [ ] Flipchart and marker pens
- [ ] Remote control car with controller
- [ ] Plastic zip-wallets and a pen (1 for each person)
- [ ] Messy-play resources for chosen activity
- [ ] Hand puppet for goodbye song

Parentplay

1. REFRESHMENTS

10 minutes Once parents have settled their children in the crèche, (this may take a little longer the first week), offer parents a chance to relax and chat amongst themselves over refreshments.

2. WELCOME

5 minutes Introduce yourselves.

Give out stickers for parents to write their names on and wear.

Explain the general housekeeping like where the toilets are, fire procedures, and any other relevant information.

3. ICE-BREAKER

5 minutes Go around the room and ask everyone, in turn, to say their name, and their children's names and ages. As they tell you how old their children are, you write the numbers up on the flipchart. At the end, you can add up the total number of years of childcare/parenting experience the group has had between them!

You may like to use a calculator for the adding up.

4. INTRODUCTION TO THE COURSE

3 minutes Tell the group why you have decided to run a Parentplay course and any relevant background about yourself and your experience as a parent/parent supporter.

Explain that you do not have all the answers and that none of us are perfect parents. But we are all doing our best and the course is designed to give the group the opportunity to learn from and encourage one another in the important job of being a parent.

5. CONFIDENTIALITY AND GROUND RULES

4 minutes Hand out the ground rules sheet, along with a plastic wallet for them to keep this and future handouts in. Read out the ground rules to the group.

We all need to agree to respect each other's confidentiality, so what is said between these four walls remains here, in order for people to feel safe in sharing their thoughts and experiences.

The only exception to this is if we were alerted to any children suffering harm. If this happens, as responsible members of society, we would have a duty to pass on information to the relevant authorities.

6.   HOPES AND ANXIETIES

10 minutes

Give each person a small cut-out yellow sun and white cloud (printed from the CD-Rom) and a pen.

Ask them to write down on the sun one thing they are hoping to gain from coming on the course and on the cloud any anxiety they may have about coming on the course.

These can then be collected and stuck onto the flipchart paper underneath the large sun (for the suns) and under the large cloud (for the small clouds) (printed from the CD-Rom).

Read out people's comments and discuss any concerns raised.

7.   SESSION AIMS AND INTRODUCTION

1 minute

This week we are going to look at how we can be ourselves, and take care of our own needs. Becoming a parent brings about change in all aspects of your life. There will obviously be good days and difficult days, but you can be sure that despite the challenges there will be times of great joy, too.

It's really important for us to remember that there is no such thing as a perfect parent, but in recognising our strengths we can use them to try to overcome our weaknesses.

8.   EMOTIONS

8 minutes

Ask parents the following question:

'How does being a parent make you feel?'

Ask the group to discuss this question as you write their answers on the flipchart. Try to include everyone and encourage quieter people to contribute.

Ideas to draw out may include: happiness, sadness, fulfilment, jealousy, frustration, excitement, fear, pride, joy, worry, anger, contentment, failure and loneliness. You may need to make a few suggestions yourself to start the group off.

These are all normal emotions: some positive, some negative. It can be hard to feel good about yourself in the midst of these emotions. There is nothing wrong with feeling these emotions but it is what we do with them that is important. There is no such thing as a perfect parent!

Parentplay

9. RECHARGING YOUR BATTERIES

5 minutes

As parents we are constantly giving out – physically, emotionally and mentally – to others. If only we could plug ourselves in overnight and recharge our batteries!

We can easily feel we are running on empty. It is at times like this that we are more likely to have less patience and less energy to cope with our children and the other demands on us.

Show the group a remote control car and demonstrate how it needs batteries and a remote control in order to work effectively. Explain that the car represents our children and the controller is us, as parents, guiding them. When both sets of batteries are fully charged, it enables both the parent and the child to get the best out of each other.

This week we will be looking at keeping our batteries charged up, and next week we will be looking at how to keep our children's batteries charged up.

---

7 minutes

Ask parents the following question:

'What drains your batteries as a parent?'

Ideas to draw out may include:

Emotional needs (guilt, self-esteem, comparing yourself with others, how we were parented ourselves, relationship difficulties)

Physical demands (lack of sleep, money pressures, tiredness, no break, time pressures)

Mental demands (juggling different jobs, stimulating your child, society's expectations of us as parents)

---

7 minutes

Divide the group into small groups of 3 or 4 people per group, and give each group paper and pens.

Ask them to discuss **'What can we do to recharge our batteries?'**

Ask groups to illustrate their answers through drawing.

Your groups may need a couple of examples to get them going, e.g. reading a book, taking a bath.

---

5 minutes

Ask someone from each group to feed back their ideas.

Draw all their feedback together and summarise with the following ideas: time to rest, time with partner, having fun, time alone.

- It is important to do something you enjoy rather than something you feel you ought to do. It's okay to have some time to yourself and time alone with your partner. We all need time to rest, relax and have fun in order to be effective parents.

- Try to draw out practical ways of taking time out. Encourage the group to think of ways they can fit relaxing and taking time out into their lives.

These suggestions will be specific to individuals, and what one person finds relaxing, could be very different to another. Ensure that everyone's ideas are respected.

Remember that it may be difficult for some people to realise that their needs are not being met and feel like there is no way out. Encourage them to make small changes one step at a time.

10.   WEEKLY HANDOUT

10 minutes

Refer to the weekly handout that was given out earlier in the session. Encourage people to spend a couple of minutes writing down what they are going to try to do at home this week.

If you have time, go round the group asking each person what they are going to put into practice this week.

11.   CONCLUSION

5 minutes

Explain the principle of messy-play time as quality time for them to spend with their children.

Let the group know which messy-play activity you will be doing today.

Collect the children from the crèche.

12.   MESSY-PLAY TIME

30 minutes

13.   GOODBYE SONG

5 minutes

Parentplay

Session 2
What's Love Got To Do With It?

Time: 2 hours

Aim:

To enable parents to explore ways of showing their children how much they love them and looking at practical ways they can demonstrate this.

Learning Outcomes:

By the end of the session participants will be able to:

1. Identify positive qualities in their children.

2. Recognise when their children's batteries are getting low.

3. Understand the importance of showing their children they are loved.

4. Know how to demonstrate various ways of showing their children that they love them.

You will need (in order of activity):

☐ Refreshments

☐ Name stickers and pens

☐ Book – *Guess How Much I Love You* by Sam McBratney

☐ Flipchart and marker pens

☐ 3-pinned plug (from an electrical appliance)

☐ Weekly handout 2 (on CD-Rom)

☐ Messy-play resources for your chosen activity

☐ Hand puppet for goodbye song

1. REFRESHMENTS

10 minutes   Once parents have settled their children in the crèche, offer parents a chance to relax and chat amongst themselves over refreshments.

2. WELCOME

1 minute   Welcome parents to this week's session.

Give out stickers for parents to write their names on and wear.

 Remember to recap on the general housekeeping like where the toilets are, fire procedures, and any other relevant information.

3. ICE-BREAKER

5 minutes

Option 1 – Ask each parent to take it in turns to write their name on a large piece of paper, in such a way that their names interlink to form a crossword. For example:

r a c h e l

m

m

a n d r e a

Option 2 – Read the story *Guess How Much I Love You* by Sam McBratney aloud to the group.

 This book will help to set the scene for the parents to think about showing their children that they love them.

4. RECAP ON LAST WEEK

10 minutes   Remind parents briefly of the key points from last week about how to take care of our own needs as well as those of our children.

 Ask if anyone would like to share what they put into action during the previous week and how it went.

 Remember to be encouraging of small steps made and give the opportunity for all to share briefly.

Parentplay

5. SESSION AIM AND INTRODUCTION

1 minute

This week we are going to look at how to show our children that we love them and how to keep their emotional batteries charged up.

6. CHILDREN'S QUALITIES

10 minutes

Ask parents the following question:

'What one thing do you like best about your child?'

Sometimes when we are having a difficult day, it is good to remember something positive about our children.

7. CHILDREN'S BATTERIES

8 minutes

Ask parents the following question:

'What behaviour would you expect from a child when their "batteries" are getting low?'

Ideas to draw out may include: crying, whining, tantrums, misbehaviour, quiet/withdrawn, noisy, overexcited.

8. KEEPING CHARGED UP

10 minutes

Divide the group into small groups of 3 or 4. Handout paper and pens to each group, and ask them to answer the following question:

'What can we do to help charge up our children's batteries?'

Ideas to draw out may include: physical needs (such as food, routine, sleep), attention (read a book together, play games, hugs and kisses, rough and tumble, make a cake together, spend one-to-one time); praise (compliment them, encourage them).

10 minutes

Ask a member of each group to feed back their ideas to the whole group.

Parentplay

9. THE 3 PS

5 minutes

Show the group a 3-pinned plug, to demonstrate that each of the pins represents one of the following words beginning with 'P'.

The following can be a positive influence to charge up children's batteries:

- Protected time
- Praise
- Positive touch

The fuller our children's batteries are, the more positive they will feel about themselves and this will, therefore, have a positive impact on their behaviour. Positive input creates positive outcome, just as negative input, creates negative output. We may not always love what they DO, but we still love THEM.

Showing our children that we love them builds their self-esteem. When they feel more positive about themselves, their behaviour is also likely to be more positive.

 It may be helpful to point out to parents that the plug can act as an everyday reminder of the 3 Ps.

10. WEEKLY HANDOUT 2

10 minutes

Give a weekly handout to each member of the group. Encourage people to spend a couple of minutes writing down what they are going to try to do at home this week.

If you have time, go round the group to ask each person what they are going to put into practice this week.

11. CONCLUSION

5 minutes

Let the group know which messy-play activity you will be doing today.

Collect the children from the crèche.

Parentplay

12. MESSY-PLAY TIME

30 minutes

13. GOODBYE SONG

5 minutes

Session 3
I'm All Ears

Time: 2 hours

Aim:

To develop parents' listening skills by gaining a better understanding of effective listening, understanding the benefits of good listening and how to put it into practice.

Learning Outcomes:

By the end of the session participants will be able to:

1. Understand the importance of listening to their children.

2. Know how to listen more effectively.

3. Use listening skills to develop their communication with their children.

You will need (in order of activity):

☐ Refreshments

☐ Flipchart and marker pens

☐ Book – *Don't Do That* by Tony Ross

☐ Copies of Agony Aunt letters (printed from CD-Rom)

☐ Weekly handout 3 (on CD-Rom)

☐ Messy-play resources for your chosen activity

☐ Hand puppet for goodbye song

Parentplay

1. REFRESHMENTS

| 10 minutes | Once parents have settled their children in the crèche, offer parents a chance to relax and chat amongst themselves over refreshments. |

2. WELCOME

| 1 minute | Welcome parents to this week's session. |
| | Give out name stickers if you feel they are still needed. |

3. RECAP ON LAST WEEK

| 7 minutes | Remind parents briefly of the key points from last week about how to show your children that you love them using the 3 Ps (protected time, praise, positive touch). |
| | Ask if anyone would like to share what they put into action during the previous week and how it went. |

 Remember to be encouraging of small steps made and give the opportunity for all to share briefly.

4. ICE-BREAKER

| 5 minutes | Read to the group the story *Don't Do That* by Tony Ross. |

 The idea of the story is to set the scene for the session and to provoke the parents to think about listening to their children.

5. SESSION AIM AND INTRODUCTION

| 1 minute | |

 This week we are going to look at understanding more about listening to our children and how to listen more effectively.

6. WHY LISTEN?

6 minutes	Divide the group into small groups of 3 or 4 to discuss the following question:
	'Why do we need to listen to our children?'
	Ask someone in each group to write down their group's comments.

5 minutes

Ask someone from each group to feed back their group's ideas.

Ideas to draw out may include:
- It makes them feel important to us, valued and loved.
- If we listen to them, they are more likely to listen to us.
- It encourages them to talk about how they are feeling and what they are thinking.
- It helps us to understand them.
- It shows that we are interested in them, and what is important to them.
- There may be something else behind what they are actually saying, e.g. a child saying, 'I don't want to go out today,' could mean they are not well, wanting attention, feeling anxious about something, etc.

7. LISTENING ROLE-PLAY

5 minutes

We have found that often people find role-play threatening. Therefore we suggest that you, as facilitators, act out the role-play below for the group to watch and then ask the questions below.

Two friends are sitting opposite each other. Ones tries to tell the other about something, e.g. about what they did that weekend.

The second person role-plays how NOT to listen, e.g. fidgeting, interrupting, yawning, looking distracted, getting up and walking around, etc.

5 minutes

Ask parents the following questions:

'How do you think the person trying to talk felt?'

Ideas to draw out may include: ignored, like giving up, cross, upset/hurt, won't talk to her again, might do the same when the friend wants to talk back to her.

5 minutes

'How could the listener have listened better?'

Ideas to draw out may include: use eye contact, physical contact, don't interrupt, pay attention, silence, don't switch off, forget own problems and listen to the talker, arrange another time to chat if it wasn't convenient then, check she has understood what her friend was saying, look interested.

Parentplay

5 minutes

'How do you think the talker would have felt if the listener had listened better?'

Ideas to draw out may include: feel important to the listener, feel valued as a person, feel loved and accepted, understood, more likely to return the favour, more likely to speak to that person again.

8. LISTENING LETTERS

15 minutes

Read out 2 or 3 of the Agony Aunt letters below.

Let each parent decide which letter they would like to answer and divide the group accordingly into 2 or 3 smaller groups.

Ask each of the groups to come up with an answer to one of the following Agony Aunt letters. (Print the letters out from the CD-Rom to give to the groups.)

Chose the letters that you feel are most suitable for your group.

Dear Aunt Ethel,

I have two children, aged 3 and 5. I work hard all day long so when I get in from work all I want to do is sit down and relax in front of the TV. My children don't understand that I need a rest and end up talking at me, jumping on me and generally winding me up. I seem to end up shouting at them, making them even worse. It has become a very stressful time of day for all of us; I've started to dread coming home.

Can you help?

Yours desperately

Ideas to draw out may include:
- *Spend some quality time with each of the children before relaxing.*
- *Explain to the children that you will spend time with them in 10 to 15 minutes' time, and make sure you stick to it.*
- *Ask partner to distract children for a while when you first get in from work.*

Dear Aunt Ethel,

I stay at home with my lovely daughter who is now 18 months old. Most of the time I really enjoy being with her, but just recently I have begun to worry about her being so demanding when I've got so much else to do around the house. She seems to want to be with me all day long, she follows me around, and isn't content to play on her own. She's at her happiest when we're chatting, reading and playing games, but I can't do that all day long! How can I still get my housework done without ignoring her?

Yours worryingly

Ideas to draw out may include:
- Chatting can be fun (even if you don't understand all her words) and could be used to teach her new things around the house.
- It may take longer to get things done but involving her in everyday activities can be important too.
- Praise her when she spends a little time without you, playing on her own.

Dear Aunt Ethel,

I'm a single parent with three kids, aged 1, 3 and 5. I love them to bits but I feel under so much pressure to make ends meet and keep everything organised. I seem to spend the whole time telling them what they should and shouldn't be doing and never get any time with them to just have fun.

Recently my eldest has begun to really misbehave, he won't listen to anything I say to him, no matter how nicely I say it. He says I never listen to him so why should he listen to me! It's making my life a nightmare. I know things need to change, but where do I start?

Yours exhaustedly

Ideas to draw out may include:
- Spend some one-to-one time with each child, starting small.
- Try to get more family time to talk, e.g. asking how their days went, over dinner.
- Try to get extra time with eldest boy.
- Try to make time during the busy day to listen if the children want to speak. It may mean things take a little longer, but it will help in the long term.
- Use good listening skills, get down on their level, make eye contact, etc.

Parentplay

Dear Aunt Ethel,

I gave up work to stay at home with my 10-month-old baby. We are getting into a routine, and practically things are beginning to get easier. The problem is that the house seems so quiet, as he's not talking yet. How can I communicate with a baby that doesn't talk back?

Yours hopefully

Ideas to draw out may include:
- Copy the sounds that he makes; use eye contact when talking to him.
- Put some music on in the background, or switch on the radio.
- Sing nursery rhymes/action songs together.
- Find a local toddler group where you can both communicate with new friends.
- Encourage his language development by commenting on what you are both doing during the day, e.g. 'We're going up the stairs', 'We're going outside', 'We're riding in the car', 'Look at the trees', etc.

9. SUMMARY

7 minutes Summarise key points from discussion groups.

Listening is a great way of giving attention to our children; as we have found out, there are advantages for us as well as them.

Our children feel more positive about themselves if we are showing them that we love them by listening to them. Children who are not listened to are more likely to get attention by using 'difficult' behaviour.

10. WEEKLY HANDOUT 3

8 minutes Give a weekly handout to each member of the group. Encourage people to spend a couple of minutes writing down what they are going to try to do at home this week.

If you have time, go around the group to ask each person what they are going to put into practice this week.

11. CONCLUSION

5 minutes Let the group know which messy-play activity you will be doing today.

Collect the children from the crèche.

Parentplay

12. MESSY-PLAY TIME

30 minutes

13. GOODBYE SONG

5 minutes

Parentplay

Session 4
It's More Than Words

Time: 2 hours

Aim:

To develop parents' awareness of how we speak to our children and to provide strategies to improve communication.

Learning Outcomes:

By the end of the session participants will be able to:

1. Understand the negative impacts of labelling children.

2. Appreciate the positive impacts of praising children.

3. Reflect on more effective communication, which does not involve shouting.

4. Understand the importance of saying sorry and how to do this practically.

You will need (in order of activity):

☐ Refreshments

☐ Bowl of sweets

☐ Flipchart and marker pens

☐ Sticky labels and pens

☐ 2 teddies, 2 dollies or 2 pictures of a child, to stick labels onto

☐ Weekly handout 4

☐ Messy-play resources for your chosen activity

☐ Hand puppet for goodbye song

1. REFRESHMENTS

8 minutes   Once parents have settled their children in the crèche, offer parents a chance to relax and chat amongst themselves over refreshments.

2. WELCOME

1 minute   Welcome parents to this week's session.

3. ICE-BREAKER

5 minutes

Pass a bowl of sweets around the room and tell people that they can choose to take 1, 2 or 3 sweets, but not to eat them yet!

Once they all have some sweets, you can ask them to tell the person next to them a number of things they like about their children, equal to the number of sweets they have taken. For example, if they have 2 sweets, then they tell 2 things that they like about their children.

4. RECAP ON LAST WEEK

7 minutes

Remind parents briefly of the key points from last week about how we can listen well to our children.

Ask if anyone would like to share what they put into action during the previous week and how it went.

 Remember to be encouraging of small steps made and give the opportunity for all to share briefly.

5. SESSION AIM AND INTRODUCTION

1 minute

This week we are going to look at how we speak to our children, and what we can change to improve this communication.

6. NEGATIVE LABELLING

It is all too easy to use words that label our children, rather than describing the behaviour itself, e.g. you naughty boy, bossy, silly…

Parentplay

5 minutes	Ask parents to give examples of labels that might be used for children and babies.

As the parents give the examples, write these onto sticky labels and stick them onto a teddy, a dolly or a large drawing of a child.

You will need to bear in mind that this subject may raise some issues for people regarding how they were brought up themselves or how they have spoken to their children in the past. Be sensitive to this and encourage parents to move on from where they are now, and direct them to where they can get further help if you feel this may be required.

You might like to take inspiration from the Mr Men/Little Miss series!

---

5 minutes

Divide the group into small groups of 3 or 4 to discuss the following question:

'How do you think this teddy/dolly/child might feel when these labels are used?'

Ask someone in each group to write down their group's comments

---

5 minutes

Ask someone from each group to feed back their ideas to the whole group.

Ideas to draw out include:
• Children will believe that they are what we tell them they are.
• Children will feel hurt.
• They may live up to what they are being called.
• They are likely to feel bad about themselves.
• They will not understand what it is, specifically, that you want them to change or how to change.
• They will think it is them that you do not like, rather than their behaviour.
• The influence of labels can continue into adulthood.

7. SPEAKING POSITIVELY

5 minutes

Ask parents to give examples of positive labels that we could use for children and babies.

As the parents give the positive examples, write these onto sticky labels and stick them onto the second teddy, dolly or large drawing of a child.

5 minutes

SMALL GROUP DISCUSSION

Divide the group into small groups of 3 or 4 to discuss the following question.

'How do you think this teddy/dolly/child might feel when these positive labels are used?'

Ask someone in each group to write down their group's comments.

5 minutes

FEEDBACK

Ask someone from each group to feed back their ideas to the whole group.

Ideas to draw out include:
- Children will believe that they are what we tell them they are.
- Children will feel built up and encouraged, building self-esteem.
- They are likely to feel good about themselves.
- The good influence of positive labels can continue into adulthood.

8. LABELLING SUMMARY

2 minutes

Explain

When we use negative labels, children are more likely to misbehave due to low self-esteem.

When we praise and encourage good behaviour this is likely to produce more good behaviour.

The way we speak to our children models how we would like them to speak to others.

9. SHOUTING SCENARIO

1 minute

Practical

Describe the following scenario:

Andrea is always really stressed. She feels as though her children never listen to her. She always seems to be shouting at them and is at the end of her tether.

10 minutes

WHOLE GROUP DISCUSSION

Ask parents the following questions:

'What impact does shouting have on Andrea's children?'

Ideas to draw out may include: fear, upset, they may get louder, become angry, it may have no effect at all if they are used to being shouted at all the time.

Parentplay

'What impact does shouting have on Andrea?'

 Ideas to draw out may include: it increases her blood pressure, makes her less able to deal with the situation, increases feelings of not being able to cope, feelings of being out of control, feelings of guilt afterwards.

'What could Andrea do differently?'

 Ideas to draw out may include:
- Plan ahead with strategies to deal with the children's behaviour when it occurs.
- Remove herself from the situation.
- Calm down.
- Distract herself.
- Distract the children.
- Try to only shout in serious situations e.g. if the children are in danger.

10. SAYING SORRY

2 minutes

 Why it is important to teach children to say sorry:

- It helps them to learn the difference between right and wrong.

- It teaches them that there are consequences to their actions.

- It is important in building relationships with people.

5 minutes

 Ask parents the following question:

'How can we teach our children to say sorry?'

 Ideas to draw out may include:
- Get down to their level or sit together.
- Make sure that they understand what they are saying sorry for, by asking them specifically, as this will help them to understand what they are doing rather than just going through the motions of saying 'sorry'.
- It may be helpful to think of different ways for young children to show that they are sorry, e.g. a 'sorry' cuddle or kiss, or by doing something helpful. It is also important to encourage them, wherever possible, to put right the consequences of what they have done, e.g. help to wipe clean the wall they've drawn on.

We can all find it difficult to say sorry but if we want to teach our children how to say sorry to others, then we need to lead by example. There will be times when we hurt or upset our children and we can choose to apologise.

11. WEEKLY HANDOUT 4

8 minutes

Give out a weekly handout to each member of the group. Encourage people to spend a couple of minutes writing down what they are going to try to do at home this week.

If you have time, go round the group to ask each person what they are going to put into practice this week.

12. CONCLUSION

5 minutes

Let the group know which messy-play activity you will be doing today.

Collect the children from the crèche.

13. MESSY-PLAY TIME

30 minutes

14. GOODBYE SONG

5 minutes

Parentplay

Session 5
Sharing Play

Time: 2 hours

Aim:

To inspire parents to enjoy sharing play with their children, by gaining a better understanding of children's play and exploring ways to join in.

Learning Outcomes:

By the end of the session participants will be able to:

1. Understand the importance of play in their child's development.

2. Know how to share and enjoy play with their children more effectively.

3. Demonstrate sharing play with their children.

4. Select a play activity to share with their child at home.

You will need (in order of activity):

☐ Refreshments

☐ Paper plates and coloured felt-tip pens

☐ Flipchart and marker pens

☐ A sheet or blanket

☐ An empty biscuit tin

☐ A basket of clothes pegs

☐ Weekly handout 5

☐ Messy-play resources for your chosen activity

☐ Hand puppet for goodbye song

1. REFRESHMENTS

10 minutes   Once parents have settled their children in the crèche, offer parents a chance to relax and chat amongst themselves over refreshments.

2. WELCOME

1 minute   Welcome parents to this week's session.

3. RECAP ON LAST WEEK

9 minutes   Remind parents briefly of the key points from last week about how talking with our children involves more than just words.

Ask if anyone would like to share what they have put into action during the previous week and how it went.

 Remember to be encouraging of small steps made and give the opportunity for all to share briefly.

4. ICE-BREAKER

5 minutes   Give each parent a paper plate and some coloured pens and ask them to draw a picture of the favourite thing or activity that they and their children enjoy playing together.

Show these to one another either by spreading them on the floor or sticking up with Blu-Tac.

5. SESSION AIM AND INTRODUCTION

1 minute

This week we are going to look at understanding more about why children play and ways in which we can have fun and join in with this, without taking over.

6. WHY PLAY

10 minutes

WHOLE GROUP DISCUSSION

Ask parents the following question:

'Why is play important?'

Parentplay

Ideas to draw out may include:
- It's how children learn.
- It allows them to explore and express their thoughts and feelings.
- It encourages imagination and creativity.
- It helps them to make sense of their lives.
- It helps them to understand and be more aware of others' feelings and ideas.
- It helps them to develop their learning in all areas: socially, physically, emotionally, mentally, and in speech and language development.
- It also helps to discover their talents, likes and dislikes.

7. WHAT DO CHILDREN NEED TO BE ABLE TO PLAY?

3 minutes

So that children can play they need:

- A safe place.

- Time and opportunity to play, both on their own and with others.

- Something to play with – not necessarily expensive toys. The simpler toys allow them to use their imagination much more, e.g. ball, cardboard boxes, pots and pans, silk scarf.

But, most importantly – YOU! Parents are the best toys children have. They are real, moving, talking toys that can listen to them and talk to them, answer questions and have fun with. Good play doesn't necessarily cost money, but it will cost you as a parent in time and interest.

8. EVERYDAY OBJECTS

4 minutes

SMALL GROUP DISCUSSION

Divide into 3 small groups.

Give each group one of the following objects: a sheet or blanket, a basket of clothes pegs, an empty biscuit tin.

Ask them to come up with 3 or 4 ideas of how they could use these items to share play with their children.

4 minutes

FEEDBACK

Ask someone from each group to feed back their ideas to the whole group.

The point that you are emphasising here is that you do not need to spend money to provide fun play activities for your children. Encourage parents to explore creative ways of using what they already have at home. Please feel free to include ideas of other everyday objects of your own in this activity.

If you have a local toy library, you could mention this here too.

9. SHARING PLAY

5 minutes

Ask parents the following question:

'What sorts of play activities could you do together?'

Ideas to draw out may include:
- At home – cooking, reading, singing nursery songs, making things, construction play, puzzles, water-play, games.
- Out and about – visit the library or park, looking at things around you, collecting things.

---

6 minutes

We have found that some people find role-play threatening, however it can be a very effective tool in expressing a point. Therefore, we suggest that the facilitators carry out the following role-play for the parents to observe and then answer the questions below:

Act out the following scenario:

One person role-plays as a child, happily playing with the pieces of a jigsaw puzzle. The child is enjoying posting the pieces into a tin and then covering the tin with a lid before putting in another one (i.e. they are playing with the pieces, not completing a puzzle).

The second person, role-playing as the parent, comes along and joins in by taking over. They help/force the child to complete the puzzle. The parent insists on using the jigsaw pieces for their intended purpose.

The end result is that the child goes off to play with something else, whilst the parent is left to complete the puzzle.

---

8 minutes

Ask the parents the following question:

'How do you think the child felt in this scenario?'

Ideas to draw out may include the following: upset, like their imaginative ideas were not good enough or important, bored, left out.

Parentpl🖐y

8 minutes

Ask parents the following question:

'What do you think the parent could have done differently?'

Ideas to draw out may include:
• Join in with the child's game, without taking over.
• Ask about what the child is doing.
• Ask if you can join in.
• Copy what they do, follow their lead.

10. WEEKLY HANDOUT 5

9 minutes

Give out a weekly handout to each member of the group. Encourage people to spend a couple of minutes writing down what they are going to try to do at home this week.

If you have time, go round the group to ask each person what they are going to put into practice this week.

11. CONCLUSION

2 minutes

Let the group know which messy-play activity you will be doing today.

Collect the children from the crèche.

12. MESSY-PLAY TIME

30 minutes

13. GOODBYE SONG

5 minutes

Session 6
Balancing With Boundaries

Time: 2 hours

Aim:

To enable parents to consider the importance of boundaries, why misbehaviour occurs and to explore strategies for managing this.

Learning Outcomes:

By the end of the session participants will be able to:

1. Understand the importance of boundaries.

2. Gain insight into the reasons behind their children's behaviour.

3. Select strategies for managing their children's behaviour at home.

4. Understand the importance of forgiveness.

You will need (in order of activity):

- [ ] Refreshments
- [ ] Flipchart and marker pens
- [ ] 3 goldfish pictures (printed from CD-ROM)
- [ ] Behaviour flowchart (on weekly handout 6)
- [ ] Post-it notes (one for each parent)
- [ ] Mega-sketcher or small wipe-board
- [ ] Weekly handout 6
- [ ] Messy-play resources for your chosen activity
- [ ] Hand puppet for goodbye song

Parentplay

1. REFRESHMENTS

10 minutes   Once parents have settled their children in the crèche, offer parents a chance to relax and chat amongst themselves over refreshments.

2. WELCOME

1 minute   Welcome parents to this week's session.

3. RECAP ON LAST WEEK

7 minutes   Remind parents briefly of the key points from last week about why children need to play and how we can join in without taking over.

Ask if anyone would like to share what they put into action during the previous week and how it went.

Remember to be encouraging of small steps made and give the opportunity for all to share briefly.

4. ICE-BREAKER

5 minutes

Read out the poem on the weekly handout about a parent's shopping trip.

This will help to set the scene for today's session. You can explain to the parents that they will have a copy of the poem at the end on their weekly handout.

5. SESSION AIM AND INTRODUCTION

2 minutes   This week we are going to look at why children behave the way they do. We are also going to look at some of the possible ways of dealing with misbehaviour. However, we're not here today to talk about the rights and wrongs of different types of punishment.

In order to deal with misbehaviour effectively we need to work out why children misbehave, then we can deal with the cause rather than just the behaviour.

6. GOLDFISH

1 minute

Giving our children boundaries allows them to enjoy freedom within a safe and loving environment, where they feel secure knowing where the limits are. The pictures of these goldfish show us how a child might feel within different types of boundaries.

9 minutes

Put the three goldfish pictures (printed from CD-ROM), onto 3 pieces of flipchart paper.

Discuss how a fish might feel in each environment.

Ideas to draw out may include:
- Goldfish in the small bowl – frustrated, trapped, alone, excluded, sad, no room for negotiation, unheard, undervalued.
- Goldfish in the normal sized fish tank – confident, happy, secure, safe, loved, cared about.
- Goldfish alone in the sea – vulnerable, unloved, lost, insecure, scared, no one cares.

Draw the analogy between the fish and how a child might feel with similar boundaries, and how different styles of discipline impact this.

Discipline means to train, teach and prepare a child for independence. When you set boundaries for your children, this is discipline; it provides the right environment for a child to learn self-control and build self-esteem.

Punishment is what happens when a child steps over the boundaries you have set. That is why it is so important that boundaries are reasonable and realistic for a child's age.

7. HOW TO *WIN* IN DISCIPLINE

10 minutes

Look together at the chart on weekly handout 6.
- It helps us to understand: **W**hy a child misbehaves
- It looks at **I**deas to deal with the misbehaviour
- It suggests what to do **N**ext.

Parentpl🖐y

Either give parents the chart or write it up on a flipchart.

Explain how to use the chart to recognise why a type of behaviour is taking place and possible strategies for dealing with it, by taking parents through the chart step by step.

As you explain the punishments, use the guidelines below.

When you use punishment you need to remember that it needs to be easy to understand, specific and consistent. Don't forget to explain to the child why they are being punished. Punishment is about the child learning that there are consequences to their actions, not about the parent expressing their anger or frustration.

Time out – without discussion, place child in a safe but boring place, for the number of minutes equivalent to their age; ignore them and allow no toys; if they move take them back again, without talking to them.

Withdrawing privileges – make sure you withdraw something that's important to them. Be realistic about what you're prepared to follow through with – don't make empty threats.

We suggest you use a couple of common examples that fit into each category, to reinforce how to use the chart.

8. HOW TO *WIN* IN DISCIPLINE – TRY IT OUT

5 minutes

Give each parent a Post-it note and pen, and explain that it is important to tackle one type of behaviour at a time.

Ask parents to write down one type of behaviour that they would like to see change in one of their children.

10 minutes

Divide into pairs.

Ask them to take it in turns to help one another to work through the chart, working out why their child is misbehaving in this way, and how they could handle the behaviour differently.

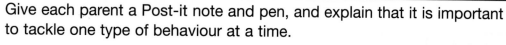
We suggest you move around and help pairs work through the chart, providing support as neccessary.

9. FORGIVENESS

5 minutes

Forgiveness is an important part of showing our children that we love them, even though we do not like what they have done. Forgiveness is a positive way for you and your children to move forward without it affecting the rest of your day.

Children need to know that they are forgiven and given a fresh start.

Demonstrate, using your mega-sketcher or wipe-board, what effect forgiveness can have.

Describe in detail an example of a typical day with young children e.g. they refuse to eat breakfast, you shout, they have a tantrum, you lose your cool, they throw their toys on the floor. For each one of the misbehaviours draw a black mark on your board.

Illustrate what happens when we say sorry and forgive each other by wiping the board clean.

We can then start again with a clean slate.

If we do not wipe the slate clean, then things between us and our children will build up, creating a difficult atmosphere that affects our relationship.

10. ENCOURAGING GOOD BEHAVIOUR

5 minutes

Divide the group into small groups of 3 or 4 to discuss the following question:

'How can we encourage more good behaviour from our children?'

5 minutes

Ask someone from each group to feed back their ideas to the whole group.

Ideas to draw out may include:
- Notice the good behaviour.
- Praise your children when they're good, kind, helpful...
- Give a smile or a hug.
- Give attention.
- Say 'well done' and be specific about what you are saying well done for.
- Sticker charts can be fun to use, too, to encourage more of the same good behaviour.

11. WEEKLY HANDOUT 6

7 minutes

Give a weekly handout to each member of the group. Encourage people to spend a couple of minutes writing down what they are going to try to do at home this week.

If you have time, go round the group to ask each person what they are going to put into practice this week.

Parentplay

Remind parents that if they are planning to put into practice strategies for discipline, they will need to discuss and agree these with their spouse/partner.

12. CONCLUSION

2 minutes   Let the group know which messy-play activity you will be doing today.

Collect the children from the crèche.

13. MESSY-PLAY TIME

30 minutes

14. GOODBYE SONG

5 minutes

Session 7
Remember, Remember!

Time: 2 hours

Aim:

To inspire parents to create positive childhood memories for their children, by understanding the importance of valuing time together and building memories.

Learning Outcomes:

By the end of the session participants will be able to:

1. Select ways of creating positive memories that they can put into practice.

2. Create a memory box for their children.

3. See the progress they have made over the weeks of the course and consider where they will go from this point.

4. Evaluate the course from their perspective.

You will need (in order of activity):

☐ Refreshments

☐ An example of a memory box with samples in it

☐ Flipchart and marker pens

☐ Weekly handout 7

☐ Evaluation forms (printed in colour from CD-ROM)

☐ Memory boxes for each child

☐ Photos for parents of their children, taken during messy-play times

and/or

☐ Laminated painted hand prints with poem (printed from CD-ROM)

☐ Messy-play resources for your chosen activity

☐ Hand puppet for goodbye song

Parentplay

1. REFRESHMENTS

8 minutes   Once parents have settled their children in the crèche, offer parents a chance to relax and chat amongst themselves over refreshments.

2. WELCOME

1 minute   Welcome parents to the final session.

3. ICE-BREAKER

8 minutes   Go around the room and ask everyone, in turn, to say what made them smile this week.

Alternatively, you could ask them to describe something that made one of their children smile this week.

4. RECAP ON LAST WEEK

7 minutes   Remind parents briefly of the key points from last week on balancing with boundaries.

Ask if anyone would like to share what they put into action during the previous week and how it went.

 Remember to be encouraging of small steps made and give the opportunity for all to share briefly.

5. SESSION AIM AND INTRODUCTION

1 minute

This week we are going to look at creating positive memories for our children.

 Remember that this week's discussions on childhood memories may be painful for some parents and you will need to be sensitive to this. Also bear in mind that some parents may feel that they have let their children down in this area and will need encouragement to make positive changes from today.

6. BUILDING POSITIVE MEMORIES

10 minutes

Ask parents the following question:

'How can we build positive memories for our children?'

 These may include ideas from some of the things that they already do. Ideas to draw out may include: days out and holidays, photos, videos, time with children as individuals, shared hobbies and interests, celebrating special days (e.g. birthdays, religious and cultural festivals), weekly events (e.g. toast in bed together on Saturdays), family traditions, remembering comical moments (e.g. when Grandma fell into the Christmas tree) or funny things children have said.

7. MEMORY BOXES

1 minute

Memory boxes can be a great way of building positive memories for children. While you cannot store feelings of love and happiness, the memories that such a box creates when looked at in years to come can help to give children a sense of being important to us and help us all to remember happy times.

1 minute

Show parents an example of a memory box but DO NOT show them what is inside yet.

6 minutes

Divide into small groups.

Ask each group to write down ten things that could be put into a child's memory box.

7 minutes

Ask someone from each group to feed back their ideas to the whole group.

 You can now open the example box to show ideas such as: ultrasound scan photos, hospital wristband, first shoes, birthday cards, postcards from holidays, first picture drawn, etc.

Parentplay

8. WEEKLY HANDOUT 7

10 minutes

Give out a weekly handout to each member of the group. Encourage people to spend a couple of minutes writing down what they are going to try to do at home this week.

If you have time, go round the group to ask each person what they are going to put into practice this week.

9. REVIEW OF THE COURSE

5 minutes

Give a brief recap on what has been covered over the past seven weeks. You can refer to the weekly handouts as a reminder.

10. EVALUATION

15 minutes

Give parents a Parentplay evaluation form and pen, giving sufficient time for the forms to be completed.

We suggest that you give out the evaluation questionnaires and then guide parents through the questions, reading it through slowly, question by question (this will particularly help any parents who may have literacy difficulties or those for whom English is not their first language).

These evaluations are essential to give you valuable feedback to help you plan your future courses.

11. CONCLUSION

5 minutes

Give parents a memory box for each of their children (or for those children who have attended the course) to take home, as a gift, to put into practice what they have learnt today.

Let the group know which messy-play activity you will be doing today.

Collect the children from the crèche.

12. MESSY-PLAY TIME

30 minutes

Parentpl🖐y

13. GOODBYE SONG

5 minutes

14. MEMENTOS

At the end, give parents photos of their children, taken during the messy-play sessions,

and/or

Give parents laminated hand prints and poem.

These can be the beginnings of their memory boxes.

 You may like to get the children to give these photos and/or hand prints to their parents. Alternatively, your hand puppet could give them out at the end of the goodbye song.

Parentplay